DEAR,

May the Almighty bless you and your family with his blessing.

The Great Four Rashidun Caliphs of Islam
The Life Story of Four Great Companions of Prophet Muhammad ﷺ

ISBN: 978-1-990544-87-3

The Rashidun Caliphate

632-661 CE

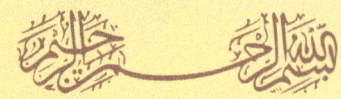

What is a Caliphate?

Before the rise of Islam, Arab tribes followed autonomous nomadic and sedentary tribal communities. After Prophet Muhammad's ﷺ first Muslim conquests, the region was politically unified and expanded under Islam. ﷺ

A caliphate is an Islamic state under the leadership of an Islamic steward with the title of 'caliph'; a person considered to be the political-religious successor of the Prophet Muhammad ﷺ and the ruler of the entire Muslim world (Ummah). Historically, the caliphates were political organizations based on Islam that developed into multi-ethnic transnational empires. During the medieval period, three main caliphates succeeded one another: The Caliphate of Rashidun (632–661), the Umayyad caliphate (661–750), and the Abbasid caliphate (750–1517). In the Fourth Great Caliphate, the Ottoman Caliphate, the rulers of the Ottoman Empire claimed caliphal authority from 1517.

Islam's first caliphate, the Rashidun Caliphate, immediately succeeded the last Messenger of Allah, Prophet Muhammad ﷺ in 632 AD. Rashidun's four caliphs were elected by the shura, a community consultation process some see as an early form of Islamic democracy.

Who is a Caliph?

Khalifah (Caliph) means successor, one who succeeds or follows someone in any position. The term was first used by Muslims, referring to Abu-Bakr al-Sidique(R.A) when he succeeded the Prophet Muhammad ﷺ in 632 AD. Abu-Bakr(R.A) was called Khalifah-tur-Rasulallah (the successor of the Apostle of God), and from that moment, the term used for all heads of the Islamic states in the Islamic golden age. The title Khalifah (Caliph) implied the functions of chief of the state. His duty was not to give new interpretations in religious matters but to adhere to the Quran and Sunnah (the practices of Rasolallah ﷺ The office of the caliphate was responsible for applying and defending Sharia' (Islamic law). Therefore, the Caliph had spiritual and worldly functions and served as a spiritual and political leader.

Abu Bakr As-Siddique

632-634 CE

Lineage and Early Life

Abu Bakr Siddique(R.A), popularly known as Abu Bakr, is the first Caliph after the Prophet Mohammad ﷺ. His full name is Abdullah bin Abu Quhafah Uthman bin Aamer Al Qurashi Al Taymi. His lineage joins with that of the Prophet ﷺ six generations before himself.

Abu Bakr Siddique(R.A) was born in Makkah in the year 573 AD (Christian Era), two years and some months after the birth of the Prophet Mohammad ﷺ. Abu Bakr(R.A) was brought up within his decent good parents; thus, he gained a considerable self-esteem and noble status. His father Uthman Abu Quhafah accepted Islam on the Day of Victory in Makkah. His mother Salma bint Sakhar, also known as Umm Al Khair, embraced Islam early and migrated to Madinah.

Abu Bakr Siddique(R.A) spent his early childhood, like other Arab children of the time, among the Bedouins. In his early years, he played with the camel calves and goats, and his love for camels earned him the nickname "Abu Bakr", meaning 'the father of the camel's calf.'

In 591 AD, at the age of 18, Abu Bakr(R.A) went into trade and adopted the profession of a cloth merchant, which was his family's business. He started his business with the capital of forty thousand dirhams and traveled extensively with caravans (camel train, series of camels carrying passengers from one place to another). Business trips took him to Yemen, Syria, and many other countries in the current Middle East. His business flourished and though his father was still alive, Abu Bakr(R.A) came to be recognized as chief of his tribe because of his many qualities such as knowledge about the history of Arabs tribes (genealogical knowledge), politics, trade/business, his kindness and many other. Even before Islam, Abu Bakr Siddique(R.A) obtained great values, high ethics, and good behaviors within the ignorant society. He was well-known among the people in Makkah as a leader over the others in morality and values. Thus, he had never been discarded or criticized for any deficiency among the Quraish tribe.

Acceptance of Islam

Abu Bakr Siddique(R.A) has accepted Islam after a long search for the true religion. When Abu Bakr(R.A) embraced Islam, the Prophet ﷺ was overjoyed, as Abu Bakr(R.A) was a source of triumph for Islam due to his intimacy with the Quraish tribe and his noble character that Allah Has exalted him.

The Holy Prophet ﷺ once said:

"Abu Bakr was the only person who accepted Islam immediately, without suspicion".

The Title of "As-Siddique"

As-Siddique, the most well-known of Abu Bakr's[(R.A)] titles, comes from the word 'Sidq', which means truthfulness. Therefore, the word As-Siddique means a person who is constantly truthful or who constantly believes in the truthfulness of something or someone. In Abu Bakr's[(R.A)] case, in the truthfulness of the Prophet Mohammad ﷺ. The title 'As-Siddique' was given to Abu Bakr[(R.A)] by none other than the Holy Prophet ﷺ.

Migration from Makkah to Madinah

When the Prophet ﷺ and his Companions (Sahaba) suffered immensely from the harm of Quraish, the Prophet ﷺ commanded his Companions to migrate to Madinah. While the Prophet's ﷺ house was besieged by a group of swordsmen from all the tribes of Makkah, he left his cousin, Ali bin Abi Talib[(R.A)], in his bed and slipped unnoticed from the house, and departed with Abu Bakr[(R.A)] in the early hours of the morning. Their journey from Makkah to Madinah was full of adventure. As soon as the besieging swordsmen discovered that they were tricked, they went in search of the Rasolallah ﷺ and Abu Bakr[(R.A)]. A public prize of a hundred camels was offered to anyone who might find them. However, it happened that when they hid in a cave named Thaur (where they spent three nights), a spider spun its web at the opening of the cave, and a pigeon built its nest there. The swordsmen followed their tracks until they reached their hiding place, but, seeing the web and the early hours of the morning, they went home, telling everyone that further pursuit was fruitless.

Allah's Messenger ﷺ once said about Abu Bakr[(R.A)]:

"No one has helped me without reciprocating it, except for Abu Bakr, who has given me help, which Allah will reciprocate to him on the Day of Resurrection. No one's property has benefited me to the extent of Abu Bakr's. And if I were to take a Khalil (friend), then I would have taken Abu Bakr as a Khalil, and indeed your companion is Allah's Khalil." (Tirmidhi: 3661)

Abu Bakr[(R.A)] had also liberated many slaves as he felt compassion for them. As per sources, he purchased and freed eight slaves, four men and four women, by paying forty thousand dinars for their freedom. Bilal bin Rabah[(R.A)], one of the most loyal and trusted companion of Prophet Mohammad ﷺ, was one of the slaves that Abu Bakr[(R.A)] freed from slavery.

The First Caliph of Islam

Abu Bakr Siddique[(R.A)], when he heard the news about the passing away of Prophet Muhammed ﷺ, he rushed towards His home. He was also shocked and felt as if a vital part of his body cut off. He reached there and kissed the forehead of Prophet Muhammad ﷺ three times and said,

"O Messenger of Allah ﷺ! Your death is as clean and graceful as your life was." (Ibn e saad)

What a dreadful day that was for all of the Companions. Every heart was sad, and each eye was shedding tears. No one was ready to accept it.

After the consultations, the day when Rasolallah ﷺ passed away, Abu Bakr[(R.A)] was elected as the first caliph of Islam in the evening. Three days earlier, Rasolallah ﷺ gave Abu Bakr[(R.A)] the charge for Islam's most important pillar, Namaz. He deserved to be the caliph as he was the closest of all companions, the friend of the cave, and the Holy Prophet's ﷺ father-in-law. He is also known as the pioneer of Islam as he was from the early converts.

Abu Bakr(R.A) went through a full year in battling against the false prophets and those who disobey Islamic government laws. Every threat had been decreased at year's end, and his position was set up in the nation.

Major Contributions

One of the most outstanding achievements Abu Bakr Siddique(R.A) rendered to Islam was the compilation of the Holy Qur'an. At that time, there were hundreds of memorizers who had memorized the entire Qur'an, but the Holy Qur'an had never been complied in a book-form. Umer bin Khattab(R.A) urged Abu Bakr(R.A) to have it written down in the form of a book. Abu Bakr(R.A) at first hesitated because this had not been done by the Holy Prophet ﷺ himself. However, after some debate on the subject, he agreed and appointed Zaid ibn Thabit(R.A) for this work. Zaid(R.A) hesitated at the thought of undertaking such a momentous task, but he later took heart and began the work. Zaid(R.A) was the most capable person to be charged with this because he had acted as a writer to the Prophet ﷺ, and one of the Companions, who had learnt the Qur'an directly from him.

Zaid ibn Thabit(R.A), said:

"By Allah, If Abu Bakr(R.A) had ordered to shift one of the mountains from its place it would not have been harder for me than what he had ordered me concerning the collection of the Qur'an."

It is reported from Ali bin Abi Talib[(R.A)], who said:

"The one who has the greatest reward amongst the people is Abu Bakr because he was unique in compiling the Qur'an."

Death and Burial Place

Abu Bakr Siddique[(R.A)] died on the 22nd of Jumada Al-Akhirah, 13th A.H. (Monday, August 23rd, 634 AD), after suffering from fever for fifteen days, during which he gave instructions that Umar bin Khattab[(R.A)] should lead the prayers. When Abu Bakr[(R.A)] died, he was sixty-three years old, and his caliphate had lasted for only two years and three months. During his illness, he was thinking of Islam and the future of the stability of the state. After consulting with many of the well-known companions of the Holy Prophet ﷺ, Abu Bakr[(R.A)] decided to confer the caliphate on Umar bin Khattab[(R.A)].

Before he died, Abu Bakr[(R.A)] gave back everything he had taken from the public treasury during his caliphate. It is said that he did not bequeath any money at all. He left only a servant, a camel and a garment. His orders were that after his death, the garment should be delivered to his successor. On seeing it, Umar[(R.A)] wept and said:

"Abu Bakr[(R.A)] has made the task of his successor very difficult."

When he died, Umar[(R.A)] led the funeral prayer, and his grave was placed adjacent to the Prophet ﷺ. Such was the peaceful death of Abu Bakr Siddique[(R.A)] after a lifelong struggle for the cause of Islam. Throughout the early years of Islam, Abu Bakr[(R.A)] was a source of comfort and constant help for the Holy Prophet ﷺ, always willing to sacrifice his wealth and his very life for the cause of Islam. After the Holy Prophet ﷺ, Abu Bakr(R.A) continued where the Prophet ﷺ had left off. He further strengthened the foundations of the Muslim nation by fighting against and defeating the apostates and then spreading Islam in some of the significant conquests during his caliphate.

May Allah be pleased with Abu Bakr(R.A) and reward him with the best of rewards. A.M.E.E.N.

عمر الفاروق رضى الله تعالى عنه

Umar Al-Farooq

634-644 CE

AL-FAROOQ

The Distinguisher Between Haq (Right) And Batil (Wrong)

Lineage and Early Life

His full name is Umar ibn Al-Khattab(R.A). He was known as Abu Hafs and earned the nickname of Al-Farooq (the Criterion) because he showed his Islam openly in Makkah, and through him, Allah(S.W.T) distinguished between disbelief and faith. He was born in 584 AD. His father was Al-Khattab ibn Nufayl, and his grandfather Nufayl was one of those whom Quraish Tribe used to refer for judgment. His mother was Hantamah bint Hashim bin Al Mugheerah.

Umar(R.A) spent half of his life in the pre-Islamic society (Jahiliyah), and grew up like his peers of Quraish, except that he has an advantage over them as the one who had learned to read, of whom there were very few. He bore responsibility at an early age and had a very harsh upbringing in which he knew no type of luxury or manifestation of wealth. His father, Al-Khattab, forced him to tend his camels.

He also excelled in many kinds of sports from his early youth, such as wrestling, riding, and horsemanship. He enjoyed and narrated poetry, and he was interested in the history and affairs of his people. Besides, he engaged in trade and profited, which made him one of the rich men of Makkah. He became acquainted with many people in the countries that he visited for trade. He traveled to Syria in the summer and Yemen in the winter. Thus, he occupied a prominent position in Makkan society during the pre-Islamic era.

Umar^(R.A) was wise, eloquent, well-spoken, strong, tolerant, noble, persuasive, and clear of speech, which made him qualified to be an ambassador for Quraish. He was an expert jurist and is best known for his justice, in the same way for Muslims and non-Muslims. This value earned him the title of 'Al- Farooq' (the one who distinguishes between right and wrong).

Acceptance to Islam

As one of the most rabid enemies of Islam and the Holy Prophet ﷺ; he was a tormentor of the Muslims, and everyone feared him.

It is said that one day, in sheer anger, Umar^(R.A) resolved to kill the Holy Prophet ﷺ and left home with this intention. As he approached the house of the Holy Prophet ﷺ, a man stopped him. When the man learned what Umar^(R.A) was up to, he told him, "Your sister and her husband have embraced Islam too. Why don't you go back to your house and set it straight!"

Hearing that, he furiously changed his direction and set out to his sister's house. As he approached their house, he could listen to the sound of the Qur'an being recited.

Umar^(R.A) walked towards the house and knocked at the door. When the sister and her husband heard the knock at the door, they hurried to hide the Book. Umar^(R.A) entered the house and demanded to know what was the humming sound he heard. His sister replied that it was the sound of them talking to each other. But Umar$^{(R.A)}$ knew well the sound of the Qur'an, so he asked them angrily.

"Have you become Muslims?"

"Yes, we have." answered the sister's husband. Umar$^{(R.A)}$ struck him in anger, and when his sister tried to defend her husband, he hit her face too. Blood started dribbling from her face by now. She stood up and faced her angry brother, saying, "You are an enemy of God! You have hit me just because I believe in Allah. Whether you like it or not, I testify that there is no god but Allah and that Muhammad ﷺ, is his slave and messenger. Do whatever you will!"

Umer$^{(R.A)}$ saw the blood running down his sister's face. Her words echoed in his ears. He demanded that the words of the Qur'an be recited to him, which he had heard as he approached the house. His sister asked him to wash clean himself up before she recited those words. He agreed and cleaned himself, and came back. When his sister recited the words from Qur'an, it filled his eyes with hot tears.

"Is this what we were up against?" he cried. "The one who has spoken these words needs to be worship." Umar$^{(R.A)}$ left his sister's house and rushed to Allah's Messenger ﷺ.

The companions accompanied the Holy Prophet ﷺ were afraid of Umar$^{(R.A)}$, so they tried to stop him.

Rasulallah ﷺ asked, "Why did you come here, son of Khattab?"

Umar(R.A) face the Holy Prophet ﷺ with humility and joy and said, "O Messenger of God! I have come for no reason except to say I believe in God and His Messenger." The Holy Prophet ﷺ was overcome with joy and cried out that Allah is great.

His conversion had a miraculous effect on the people of Makkah, and more and more people now started to accept the message of the Holy Prophet ﷺ.

Umar(R.A) lived during the pre-Islamic era and knew it inside out. He knew its true nature, customs, and traditions, and he defended it with all the power he possessed. Therefore, when he entered Islam, he understood its beauty and true nature, and he recognized the great difference between guidance and misguidance, disbelief and faith, truth and falsehood.

Migration From Makkah to Madinah

When Umar(R.A) decided to migrate to Madinah, he insisted on doing it openly. Ibn Abbas(R.A) said:

"Ali bin Abi Talib(R.A) said to me: 'I do not know of any of the migrants who did not migrate in secret, except Umar ibn Al-Khattab. When he decided to migrate, he put on his sword, put his bow over his shoulder, picked up his arrows, and carried his stick. He went out to the Ka'bah, where a number of Quraish were gathered in its courtyard. He said to them, 'May your faces become ugly! Allah will only rub these noses in the dust. Whoever wants his mother to be bereft of him and his children to become orphans and his wife to become a widow, let him meet me behind this valley.' Ali(R.A) said, 'No one followed him.'"

The Successor of Caliph Abu Bakr^(R.A)

When Abu Bakr's^(R.A) sickness grew intense, the people gathered around him, and he said:

"Your affairs are in your hands, so appoint over you whomever you like. If you appoint someone whilst I am still alive, I think it is less likely that you will become divided after I am gone."

Hence, they came back to him and said:

"We have decided to leave it to you, O' Successor of the Messenger of Allah 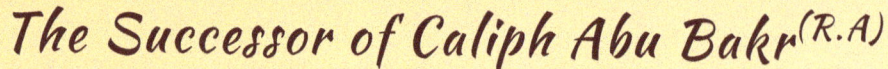."

He said: "Give me time so that I may choose someone who will be most pleasing to Allah, and most protective of His religion and His slaves."

So, he looked out over the people and said to them:

"Do you accept the one whom I appoint as your leader? By Allah, I have tried to appoint the best; I have not appointed a relative. I have appointed Umar ibn Al-Khattab as your leader, so listen to him and obey."

The companions said: "We will listen and obey."

Then Abu Bakr^(R.A) turned in supplicating to Allah^(S.W.T), expressing his concern to his Lord. He said:

"I have appointed over them the best of them and the one who is keenest to lead them in the right way."

Umar (R.A) as Caliph

He was the first caliph to be nominated as "Ameer-ul-Momineen (Prince of the Believers)". His achievements, during his reign as Caliph, are so many, however, following are some highlights of his accomplishments during the tenure of his 'Khilafat':

- He is the one who founded the Lunar Calendar (Hijri Year i-e according to the date of Prophet Mohammad's ﷺ migration to Medinah).
- In his era, Islam gained a great position, as the Islamic Empire expanded at an unprecedented rate ruling the whole Iraq, Egypt, Libya, Tripoli, Persia, Khurasan, Eastern Anatolia, South Armenian, and Sajistan. Jerusalem (first Qiblah) was conquered during his reign along with the whole Sassanid Persian Empire and two-thirds of the Eastern Roman Empire.
- He introduced and implemented different Political and Civil administration jobs such as Chief Secretary (Khatib), Military Secretary (Khatib-ud-Diwan), Revenue Collector (Sahib-ul-Kharaj), Police Chief (Sahib-ul-Ahdath), Treasury Officer (Sahib Bait-ul-Maal), and many other official posts.
- Umar (R.A) was the first to establish a special department to investigate complaints against the officers of the State.
- He also introduced the practice of measuring the land and keeping its record, adopted a census system. He had canals dug and populated cities like Koofah, Basrah, Jeezah, Fustat (Cairo) and delineated provinces out of the conquered territories.
- He was the first to allow traders of rival countries to enter Muslim territories for the purpose of business.

- Umar[R.A] was the first to introduce the public ministry system, where officials' and soldiers' records were kept. He was also the first person ever to appoint police forces to maintain civil order. Another important aspect of Umar's[R.A] rule was that he banned any of his governors/officials from engaging in trade or any business dealings while being in a position of power.

- Above all, in the conquered lands, Umar[R.A] did not demand that non-Muslim populations convert to Islam, nor did he attempt to centralize the government. Instead, he allowed the conquered populations to retain their religion, language, and customs and left his rule relatively intact, imposing only one governor (Amir) and one financial agent (Amil). These new positions were an integral part of the efficient fiscal network that financed the empire.

Umar's[R.A] general instructions to his officers were:

"Remember, I did not appoint you as commanders and tyrants over the people. Instead, I sent you out as leaders so that people would follow you. Give Muslims their rights so they won't be abused. Praise them not excessively, lest they fall into the sin of vanity. Do not close the doors on their faces; otherwise, the more powerful would eat the weak. And don't act like you're superior to them because it's tyranny over them."

Martyrdom

Imam ibn Kathir said that when Umar(R.A) concluded his rites of Hajj in 23 Hijri, he prayed and asked Allah(S.W.T) to take him to Himself and to grant him martyrdom in the land of the Holy Prophet 🕌, i.e., Madinah. Allah is indeed kind to whom He wishes. It happened that Abu Lulu Al- Fayruz, the Magian (the fire worshiper), a nonbeliever and had a Roman origin, stabbed Umar(R.A) while he was in the Fajr Salah (dawn prayer) with a dagger of two blades. He stabbed him three times, one of these below the naval. Hence, Umar(R.A) fell bleeding copiously and was taken to his house with blood gushing out from his wound. All of these occurred before sunrise.

Then Umar(R.A) asked: "Who killed me?"

His companions replied, "Abu Lulu, the Magian."

Then Umar(R.A) was delighted and said: "Praise be to Allah who Has not afflicted me from the hands of someone who subscribes to monotheism. I used to forbid you from sending us any uncouth infidel, but you disobeyed me."

Then he said: "Call for my brothers."

They asked: "Who?"

Umar(R.A) said: "Uthman, Ali, Talhah, Zubair, Abdul Rahman bin Awf, and Sad bin Abi Waqas."

When they arrived, Umar(R.A) said:

"I have looked into the affairs of the Muslims, and I found you six the foremost and the smart. I do not see the authority fitting for anyone except one of you. If you are upright, then the affair of the people will be upright. If there is disagreement, it is because you had disagreed (amongst yourselves)." His blood was mopped for him, and he said: "Consult for three days, and in the meantime, Suhayb Ar-Rumi should lead the people in prayer." They asked: "Who should we consult with, O' Prince of believers?" He replied: "Consult with the Immigrants and the Supporters as well as the commanders of the armies."

He requested for a drink of milk. When he drank it, the whiteness of the milk could be seen oozing out from his wounds, and it was clear for them that he would die. He said:

"The time is now (i.e., of death). If I were to have the entire world, I would have given it out to ransom myself from the horror of the point of departure."

Then, his soul was taken. This happened on 26 Dhul Hijjah, 23 A.H. (Wednesday 7th of November 644 AD). He was sixty-three years old and his era extended for ten years.

As per Umar's[R.A] will, he was buried, with the permission of the Mother of the believers, Aisha Siddiqua[R.A], alongside the Prophet Mohammad ﷺ and Caliph Abu Bakr[R.A] in Masjid Al-Nabawi.

The Austerity of Umar[R.A]

Umar[R.A] was most humble to Allah and led an austere life. His food was very coarse, and he would patch his cloth with leather. He used to carry a water skin on his shoulders despite his great esteem. He seldom laughs and never joked with anyone. Engraved on his ring was: "Death is sufficient as an admonition, O' Umar."

When he was appointed as the Caliph, he said: "Nothing is permissible (for me) from the treasury more than two clothes, one for the cold season and the other for the dry season. The sustenance of my family will be the equivalent of an average man of Quraish and not the rich amongst them, for I am just an ordinary man among the Muslims (i.e., nothing special about me)."

On the historic mission to Jerusalem, a bag full of parched barley meal, a camel, a slave, and a wooden cup were all the belongings of Umar[R.A], the Khalifah of the Muslim Ummah, a magnificent and powerful Islamic ruler whose cavalry had already trampled down palaces and crowns and thrones under the hooves of its horses. It was a unique scenario of Islamic equality and human dignity that at times the Caliph sat on the camel, and the slave walked along holding the rein of the camel and at other times, vice versa.

At the time of drought, Umar[R.A] ate bread and oil until his skin turned pale dark, and he would say: "What a bad leader I am if I eat my fill and the people go hungry."

May Allah reward him with the best of rewards. A.M.E.E.N.

Usman Zun-Noorain

644-656 CE

Lineage and Life before Islam

His full name is Uthman ibn Affan[R.A]. He was born in Makkah, and he was about five years younger than the Allah's Apostle ﷺ. His father died before Islam, i.e., the pre-Islamic period. His mother's name was Arwa bint Kurayz, and she died in the era when Usman[R.A] was caliph. In the pre-Islamic society, Uthman[R.A] was among the best of his people. He was of high status, very wealthy, too modest, and eloquent in speech. His people loved him dearly and respected him. He never prostrated to any idol and had never committed any immoral action even before Islam. He also did not drink alcohol before Islam. He was well versed in the knowledge of lineages, proverbs, and the history of important events. He travelled to Syria and Ethiopia and mixed with non-Arab people, learning things about their lives and customs that no one else knew. He took care of the business that he had inherited from his father, and his wealth grew. He was regarded as one of the men of Banu Umayyah clan who were held in high esteem by all of Quraish. Thus, Uthman[R.A] was regarded as being of high status among his people, and he was loved dearly.

Acceptance of Islam &
Immense love with Rasulallah ﷺ

Uthman(R.A) was thirty-four years old when Abu Bakr As-Siddique(R.A) called him towards Islam, and he did not hesitate at all and responded immediately to the call of Abu Bakr(R.A). He was the fourth man to embrace Islam after Abu Bakr(R.A), Ali ibn Talib(R.A) and Zaid ibn Harithah(R.A). He became Muslim early and participated in the two Migrations: first to Abyssinia (Ethiopia) and then Madinah.

The most vital factor that boosted Uthman's(R.A) character, which brought out his talents and potentials, and purified his soul, was his keeping company with the Messenger of Allah ﷺ and studying at his hands. He said:

"Allah Almighty sent Prophet Mohammad ﷺ with the truth and revealed the Book to him, and I was one of those who responded to Allah and His Messenger ﷺ and believed. I made the two early migrations, and I became the son-in-law of the Messenger of Allah ﷺ, and I received guidance directly from him".

He was one of the ten given glad tidings of paradise by the Prophet Muhammad ﷺ and one of the Companions who compiled the Quran.

Love of Qur'an

Uthman^(R.A) was deeply attached to the Holy Qur'an. He was a 'Hafiz' of the Qur'an (memorization of Qur'an) and used to read the Qu'ran all the time. Uthman^(R.A) recited the entire Qur'an back to Prophet Mohammad ﷺ before he passed away.

It was narrated that:

"Those who taught the Qur,an such as Uthman ibn Affan, Abd-Allah ibn Masood, and others, told us that when they learned ten verses from the Holy Prophet ﷺ, they would not go beyond them until they had learned the knowledge contained in them and how to apply it in deeds."

Following sayings of Uthman^(R.A) clearly show his attachment and love for the Holy Qur'an:

"If our hearts were pure, we would never have our fill of the words of Allah^(S.W.T)"

"I would not like the day to come when I do not look in the Book of Allah (i.e., The Holy Qur'an)."

Migration to Ethiopia

Uthman^(R.A) and his wife Syeda Ruqayyah^(S.A), daughter of the Holy Prophet ﷺ, migrated to Ethiopia (Abyssinia) along with ten Muslim men and three women. Some Muslims later joined them as migrants. All emigrant Muslims found safety, security, and freedom of worship in Abyssinia. Uthman^(R.A)

already had some business contacts in Ethiopia; therefore, he continued to practice his profession as a trader.

When there was a rumor that the people of Makkah had become Muslims, news of that reached the emigrants in Abyssinia, so they came back, but when drew close to Makkah, they heard that the news was false. Nevertheless, all emigrants entered the city. Among those who returned were Uthman(R.A) and Syeda Ruqayyah(S.A) and they re-settled in Makkah. Uthman(R.A) remained in Makkah until Allah granted permission to migrate to Madinah.

Marriage with the Daughters of Rasulallah ﷺ

He married Syeda Ruqayyahh(S.A), daughter of the Prophet Mohammad ﷺ, who passed away on the night of Battle of Badr. When the Muslims went out to fight the Battle of Badr, Uthman's(R.A) wife was sick and was confined to her bed at the time when his father, Prophet Mohammad ﷺ, called on the Muslims to intercept the caravan of Quraish. Uthman(R.A) hastened to go out with the Messenger of Allah ﷺ, but he ﷺ did not allow Uthman(R.A) to go with them and ordered him to stay with Ruqayyah(S.A) and nurse her by saying:

"You [Uthman(R.A)] will receive the same reward and share (of the booty) as anyone of those who participated in the battle of Badr (if you stay with her)." (Bukhari: 3699)

Uthman(R.A) obeyed willingly and stayed with his wife. When she breathed her last breaths, she was longing to see her Father ﷺ, but she did not get to see him. Her grieving husband, Uthman(R.A), buried his beloved wife in Al-Baqee (the sacred graveyard of Muslims near Masjid Al-Nabawi in Madinah). After returning victorious from the Battle of Badr, Rasulallah ﷺ learned about his daughter's death. He went out to Al-Baqee and stood over her grave and prayed for forgiveness.

After the death of Syeda Ruqayyah (S.A), Prophet Mohammad ﷺ married his other daughter, Syeda Umm Kulthom (S.A), with Uthman (R.A). As narrated by Abu Hurairah (R.A), the Messenger of Allah ﷺ stood at the door of Masjid Al-Nabawi and said:

"O Uthman, Jibreel has told me that Allah wants you to marry Umm Kulthoom for a dowry (Mehr) similar to that of Ruqayyah and to treat her with similar kindness." (Ibn Majah: 110)

Uthman (R.A) and Syeda Umm Kulthoom (S.A) got married. After three days of their marriage, Prophet Mohammad ﷺ paid a visit to her daughter and asked:

"O my daughter, how did you find your husband (i.e., Uthman)?" She said: "The best of husbands."

Umm Kulthoom (S.A) stayed with Uthman (R.A) until her death. Prophet ﷺ offered the funeral prayer for her. Uthman (R.A) was deeply grieved by the loss of Syeda Umm Kulthoom (S.A). When Rasulallah ﷺ saw Uthman (R.A) walking broken-hearted with signs of grief on his face and He ﷺ came to Uthman (R.A) and said:

"O Uthman, if I had a third one, I would give her in marriage to you."

This is inductive of the love of the Prophet Mohammad ﷺ for Uthman (R.A), and of Uthman's (R.A) loyalty and respect towards his Prophet ﷺ. The scholars say that no one is known to have married two daughters of a Prophet except him. For this reason, he was nicknamed 'Zun-Noorain' (the one with the two lights).

Contribution for the spread of Islam And Muslim's Welfare

Uthman(R.A) was one of the richest of those on whom Allah Had bestowed wealth. He used his wealth in the obedience of Allah(S.W.T) He always was the first to do good and spend in the way of Allah(S.W.T), and he did not fear poverty. Among the many examples of his spending are the following:

- When the Prophet ﷺ came to Madinah, the only source of fresh water was the well of Bir Rumah, and without payment, no one allowed to drink water from the well. Uthman(R.A) bought the well from the owner (who was a jew) for twenty-thousand dirhams and donated it for the rich and poor and wayfarers.
- In Madinah, Masjid Al-Nabawi became too small for the Muslims to pray five times. Uthman(R.A) bought the land next to the mosque for twenty-five or twenty thousand dirhams, and this land was added to the mosque, which then became large enough to accommodate the Muslims.
- He spent a significant amount on equipping the Muslim army for the campaign of Tabook.
- During the caliphate of Umar(R.A), the status of Uthman(R.A) was that of adviser. During Umar(R.A) caliphate, Uthman(R.A) set-up the system of keeping records of wealth spent and earned (the Diwan). Uthman(R.A) was the one who suggested to Umar(R.A) that he should make the Hijri Year (Islamic Calendar).

Appointment as Caliph

Umar ibn Al-Khattab[(R.A)], on his death bed, formed a committee of six people to choose the next Caliph from amongst themselves. The committee narrowed down the options to two: Uthman[(R.A)] and Ali[(A.S)]. Ali[(A.S)] was from the Banu Hashim clan (the same clan as Prophet Muhammad ﷺ) from the Quraish tribe, and he was also the cousin and son-in-law of the Holy Prophet ﷺ and had been one of his companions from the start of his preaching. Uthman[(R.A)] was from the Banu Umayya Clan of Quraish tribe. He was a second cousin and son-in-law of the Prophet Muhammad ﷺ and one of the first converts to Islam. So, Ali[(R.A)] voted for Uthman[(R.A)] and Uthman[(R.A)] voted for Ali[(R.A)].

Uthman[(R.A)] was ultimately chosen. On the fourth day, after the death of Umar[(R.A)], Uthman[(R.A)] was elected as the third Caliph with the title 'Amir Al-Muminin' (The Prince of the Believers). He stood before the people and declared his approach to ruling, explaining that he would follow the guidelines of the Qur'an and Sunnah, and follow the footsteps of the two predecessors Caliphs [i.e., Abu Bakr[(R.A)] and Umar[(R.A)]]. He also stated that he would run the people's affairs with forbearance and wisdom, but he would accept no compromise concerning punishments that must be carried out for justice.

Highlights of His Reign as Caliph

Uthman's[R.A] achievements during his reign as Caliph, are so many. He ruled for twelve years. Following are some highlights of his accomplishments during the tenure of his Caliphate (Khilafat):

- Conquest: Uthman[R.A] continued the wars of conquest started by Umar[R.A]. Rashidun's army conquered North Africa from the Byzantines and even took Spain, conquering the coastal areas of the Iberian Peninsula, as well as the islands of Rhodes and Cyprus. Also, Rashidun's army completely conquered the coast of Sicily, the Sassanid Empire, and its eastern borders extended as far as the Indus River.

- Expansion of Prophet's Mosque: Uthman[R.A] expanded the Prophet's Mosque (Masjid Al-Nabawi) in 29-30 A.H. and has established the first Islamic fleet to protect the Muslim beaches from the attacks of Byzantines.

- Compilation of the Qur'an: One of the most significant achievements of Uthman[R.A] is the compilation of the Holy Qur'an, which was started in the caliphate of Abu Bakr Siddique[R.A]. Under his authority, diacritics were written in Arabic letters so that non-native Arabic speakers could easily read the Quran.

In the latter half of his caliphate, due to the expansion of Islamic conquests and new Muslims who did not absorb the spirit of order and obedience and enemies of Islam led by Jews started to provoke civil conflict to weaken the unity of Muslims and their state. They raise doubts about the policy of Uthman[R.A] and incited the people in Egypt, Kufa, and Basra to rebellion. They deceived their followers into implementing their plan and met the caliph and asked him to give up. Uthman(R.A) called them to the meeting in the mosque with senior companions(R.A) and other people of the city. He refuted their unreliable gossips, and he answered their questions but pardoned them. Thus, they returned to their country concealing their malice and swore to come back to the city to carry out their conspiracies, which were exaggerated by the Jew Abdullah bin Saba, who pretended to be a Muslim.

Martyrdom

In Shawwal, 35 A.H., the turmoil occurred, and the wrong-doers besieged Uthman(R.A) in his home for forty days and prevented him from praying in the mosque and even from water. But when he saw some of the Companions(R.A) that had prepared to fight them, he prevented that fight as he did not want to drop the blood of a Muslim for his own sake. Then the conspirators broke into his house from the back and attacked him as he was reading the Holy Qur'an. His wife Naila(R.A) attempted to protect him, but they beat her with the sword, cutting off her fingers. The rebels killed him, and his own treasured copy of the Qur'an was soaked with his blood. He was martyred on the 18th of Dhul-Hijjah 35 Hijri, 656 AD. He was buried at Al-Baqee, the sacred graveyard of Muslims near Masjid Al-Nabawi in Madinah.

May Allah have mercy on Uthman ibn Affan(R.A) and be pleased with him and assemble us among his company. A.M.E.E.N.

Ali Asadullah

656–661 CE

ASADULLAH
The Lion Of Allah

Lineage & Attributes

His full name is Ali Ibn Abi Talib. He came from the most respectable family of the Quraish tribe, Banu Hashim's family, and he was the cousin of the Prophet Muhammad ﷺ. His mother's name was Fatimah(R.A), and she embraced Islam early and migrated to Madinah. His father, Abu Talib was chief of the Banu Hashim tribe, and he was the custodian of the Ka'ba and was the uncle of the Prophet Muhammad ﷺ. Abu Talib was a descendant of the Prophet Ismael(A.S), the son of Prophet Ibrahim(A.S).

Ali(A.S) was born in Makkah, and he embraced Islam so early when he was nine years of age. He was one of the ten men given the glad tidings of Paradise. He married the Prophet's ﷺ daughter Syeda Fatima(S.A). He was a prominent scholar, a courageous soldier, a notable ascetic, and a remarkable orator.

Early life and Acceptance of Islam:

When Ali(A.S) was at the age of five, Quraish was struck with a drought that affected the economic status in Makkah. Hence, the Holy Prophet ﷺ appealed to his uncle Al-Abbas to help Abu Talib during the crisis. They offered Abu Talib to care for his children, as Al-Abbas chose to care for Jafar, and the Holy Prophet ﷺ took Ali(A.S) and gave him every kindness and affection in his early childhood, which influenced him for the rest of his life. He grew up in the household of the Holy Prophet ﷺ, and when the Holy Prophet ﷺ received the first revelation, Ali(A.S) was the first to become Muslim in early childhood.

Once Ali ibn Abu Talib(R.A) came back home while the Prophet ﷺ and his noble wife Khadijah(R.A) were praying. Ali(R.A) asked about the prayer, then the Prophet ﷺ told him that it is the right religion that demands worshiping no god but Allah. But the Prophet ﷺ asked him to keep the matter in secret. The next morning Ali(R.A) came to the Prophet ﷺ and declared his Islam. In the beginning, he kept his Islam a secret, fearing from his father, but when Abu Talib recognized him, he approved and asked him to sustain to it.

Role in the Holy Prophet's ﷺ Migration from Makkah to Madinah

The Prophet Muhammad ﷺ was well-known as the most trustworthy of men in Makkah. Although they did not accept his religion, the people of Makkah continued to trust him regarding their precious stuff and money in his safe-keeping. At the initial stage of Islam, Muslims faced immense hardships by the nonbelievers of Makkah. The Prophet Muhammad ﷺ remained in Makkah waiting for Allah's permission to migrate to Madinah while his Companions migrated early. When disbelievers of Makkah plotted to kill the Messenger of Allah ﷺ, the Angle Gabriel(A.S) revealed to him the details of that evil conspiracy. So, the Holy Prophet ﷺ asked Ali(A.S) to sleep in his bed to impersonate him, confusing the killers that the Holy Prophet ﷺ is still in the house; while He left his house safely at night and migrated to Madinah along with Abu Bakr Siddique(R.A). It was Ali(A.S) whom the Holy Prophet ﷺ trusted to return the possessions to their owners when he left for Madinah. Later, Ali(A.S) also migrated to Madinah to join the Holy Prophet ﷺ. Ali(A.S) had suffered immensely in his journey to Madinah, as he spent that long journey walking on his feet. As he reached Madinah, Rasulallah ﷺ met him gladly, sending faithful prayers to Allah(S.W.T) and seeking goodness and blessings for Ali Ibn Abi Talib(A.S).

After the migration to Madinah, when the Holy Prophet ﷺ laid down the foundations of the Islamic society, Ali(A.S), being so close to him, was extremely active in serving the Holy Prophet ﷺ, following his orders and learning from his guidance.

Marriage with Syeda Fatima(S.A)

Ali(A.S) married the Holy Prophet's ﷺ most beloved daughter, Syeda Fatima (s.a.), one of the best women all over. Her mother was Khadijah(R.A). The blessed marriage took place in Madinah after the Battle of Ohud. Thus, Ali(A.S) had the additional honor of being the father of the Prophet Muhammad's ﷺ progeny through his sons, Al-Hasan(A.S) and Al-Hussain(A.S), and daughters, Zainab(A.S), and Umm Kulthoom(A.S), from Syeda Fatima (s.a.).

Contributions and Support in the spread of Islam

Ali(A.S) was so reliable and trustworthy that the Holy Prophet ﷺ designated him as one of the scribes who would write down the text of the Holy Qur'an, which had been revealed to him during his lifetime. As Islam began to spread throughout Arabia, Ali(A.S) helped establish the new Islamic order by carrying the messages and declaring the Islamic guidelines. Further, he was instructed to write down the Treaty of Hudaybiyah, the peace treaty between the Prophet Muhammad ﷺ and Quraish. Ali(A.S) was sent to Yemen to spread the teachings of Islam. He was also charged with settling several disputes and putting down the revolts of various tribes.

The Lion of Allah(S.W.T)

Ali(A.S) was well known for his bravery. He participated in almost all the battles against the nonbelievers during the time of the Prophet Muhammad ﷺ, except for the Battle of Tabuk in the year of 9th Hijri, as the Holy Prophet ﷺ had placed Ali(A.S) in charge of the city. He also took part in individual battles against the nonbelievers and dominated Arabia's most famous warriors. As well as being the standard-bearer in those battles, Ali(A.S) led parties of warriors on raids into enemy lands.

At the Battle of Badr, he defeated the Umayyad champion, Walid Ibn Utba, and twenty other polytheist soldiers.

Ali(A.S) was prominent at the Battle of Uhud when the standard-bearer of Islam was martyred; it was Ali(A.S) who raised it up. Then, he was challenged by an unbeliever whom Ali(A.S) fought and defeated single-handedly. It was Ali(A.S) too, who drew around the Holy Prophet ﷺ with other loyal Companions, when the archers deserted their spots in quest of booty and the chaos happened. Ali(A.S), whom Allah Had protected, stood steadfast beside the Prophet Muhammad ﷺ.

In the Battle of the Trench, Ali(A.S) courageously defeated a prominent leader of the unbelievers called Amr Ibn Wudd.

In the Battle of Khaybar, when the Muslim army failed to conquer the Jewish fortress twice, the Holy Prophet ﷺ said that night: "By God, tomorrow I shall give it [the banner] to a man who loves God and His Messenger, and whom God and His Messenger love. Allah will bestow victory upon him." The next morning, the companions brought Ali(A.S) along, but he had sore eyes (ophthalmia). They took him to the Messenger of Allah (ﷺ), who applied his saliva to his eyes, and he got well. The Messenger of Allah (ﷺ) gave him the banner.

When Ali(A.S) reached the Citadel of Qamus, he was met at the gate by Marhab, a Jewish chieftain who was well experienced in battle. Marhab called out: "Khaybar knows well that I am Marhab, a tested valorous warrior, whose weapon is sharp. Sometimes I thrust with the spear; sometimes I strike with the sword; when lions advance in a burning rage".

Ali(A.S) chanted in reply:

"I am the one whose mother named him 'Haidar (Lion)', (And am) like a lion of the forest with a terror-striking countenance. I give my opponents the measure of sandara in exchange for sa' (goblet) i. e. return their attack with one that is much fiercer)."

The two soldiers struck at each other, and after the second blow, Ali(A.S) cleaved through Marhab's helmet, splitting his skull and landing his sword in his opponent's teeth. Another narration described, "Ali(A.S) struck at the head of Mirhab and killed him." During the battle, a Jew struck him so that his shield fell from his hand, and Ali(A.S) lost his shield. In need of a substitute, he picked up a door and used it to defend himself. The door was said to be so heavy that it took eight men to replace it on its hinges. It is also said that, when the time came to breach the fortress, he threw the door down as a bridge to allow his army to pass into the citadel and conquer the final threshold. The fortress fill to the onslaught of the Muslims, and victory attained.

Additionally, Ali(A.S) was one of the Companions who stood unwavering beside the Prophet Muhammad ﷺ in the Battle of Hunain.

The title of "the Lion of Allah(S.W.T)" is well deserved for Ali ibn Abi Talib(A.S) for his valor on the battlefields.

Support to the first three Caliphs

Abu Bakr As-Siddique(R.A) sent Ali(A.S) with a group of the Companions to protect the borders of the city in critical times. In addition, Abu Bakr(R.A) consulted Ali(A.S) before fighting apostasy and the Romans. Narrations revealed that judgeship was delegated to Ali(A.S) during Abu Bakr's caliphate(R.A).

Ali(A.S) pledged his allegiance to Umar(R.A) and helped him as a trusted advisor. Under the caliphate of Umar(R.A), a unique period in the history of the world in terms of territorial conquest, Ali a.s) was entitled to the post of advisor to the Caliph. No major issue has been resolved without his consultation. By his courage and bravery, he stood out among his contemporaries. During the caliphate of Umar(R.A), the Islamic army conquered the Roman Emperor in Syria, Egypt, and North Africa. Additionally, the Islamic army conquered the Persian Emperor in Iraq, Persia, Khurasan, extending to the borders of Turkey and India. All the way through, Umar(R.A) used to consult the wise Companions of the Prophet ﷺ such as Ali(A.S), and seek their suggestions in political issues. It was narrated that Ali(A.S) was the one who advised Umar(R.A) to set Hijra as the beginning of the Islamic calendar. Also, it was Ali(A.S) who advised Umar(R.A) to go to Jerusalem in order to receive the Holy Mosque from the Romans, while Umar(R.A) placed Ali(A.S) in charge of Madinah. Thus, it is he who succeeds in seizing the citadel of Khalibar. Ali(A.S) was one of Umar's electoral councils(R.A) to choose the third caliph. Uthman(R.A) and Ali(A.S) were the two major candidates.

Ali(A.S) also pledged his allegiance to Uthman(R.A) and remained in Madinah to support him. Ali(A.S) represented a considerable role during the incitement to rebellion against Uthman(R.A). Ali(A.S) supported Uthman(R.A) and defended him by offering advice and facing the provincial opposition coming from Egypt and Iraq. They aimed at displacing Uthman(R.A) with Ali(A.S), but the latter resolutely rejected their demands. Thus, they pretended to be retreating, but after three days, they returned to Madinah to besiege Uthman(R.A) and his family. Ali(A.S) and his sons defended Uthman(R.A) ardently, and they were intended to fight the rebellious, but Uthman(R.A) refused to kill people for his sake. It was a complicated misfortune in Islamic history, marked by the murder of Uthman(R.A).

Ali Ibn Abi Talib(A.S) As The Fourth Caliph

After the martyrdom of the third Caliph, Uthman(R.A), Prophet's Companions approached Ali(A.S), asking him to be the Caliph. First, he has declined the responsibility of this great office, suggesting to be a counselor instead of a chief. But finally, he decided to put the matter before the Muslims in the Prophet's Mosque. As a result, the overwhelming majority of the Companions in Madinah considered Ali(A.S) to be the most suitable person to be the Caliph after Uthman(R.A). Also, on the occasion of the election of third caliph, the final choice was between Uthman(R.A) and Ali(A.S). Uthman(R.A) had voted in favor of Ali(A.S) and Ali(A.S) in favor of Uthman(R.A) as the most suitable person for the office of the caliphate. Ali(A.S) was considered the ideal man for the fourth caliph. If he couldn't have stopped the inevitable course of events, neither could anyone else. In fact, however, it turned out to be the best possible solution for the good of Islam in these stormy days. As for judgment, he had no equal among the companions of the Holy Prophet ﷺ. Thus, he agreed to take the responsibility, and pledges of loyalty were sworn to him.

Several problems faced the new Caliph when he took power. Firstly, he has to establish peace in the state and amend the deteriorating political situation. Secondly, he needed to take action against the assassins of Uthman(R.A). Shortly after Ali(A.S) became caliph, he removed the provincial governors who had been appointed by Uthman(R.A) and replaced them with trusted aides. He wrote instructions to his officials that clarify what form of the regime he wanted to introduce. Ali(A.S) told people that Muslim politics had become plagued with disagreement and disharmony and that he wanted to purge Islam of any evil it had suffered. He then warned all concerned that he would not tolerate any rebellion and that all those convicted of rebellious activities would be treated harshly. He advised people to behave like true Muslims. It was not going to be a regime in which the officers dominated and got fat on public money. He believed that people and rulers had rights over each other, and Allah(S.W.T) created these rights in such a way that they were equal to each other. It would be a regime where the governed and the taxpayers would have a premium. It was their convenience that the state had to work. It was a welfare state that worked only for the welfare of the people who lived under its rule, a regime in which the rich cannot get richer while the poor get poorer; a regime where the canons of religion strike a balance between the ruled and the rulers.

The reign of Ali(A.S) was notably marked by the occurrence of tests and troubles among Muslims. Careful reading in Islamic history revealed that the main cause of those troubles was the Sabites party, supported by fled slaves and village dwellers. Their leader, Abdullah ibn Saba, was a jew but pretended conversion to Islam during the caliphate of Uthman ibn Affan(R.A). The main goal of Ibn Saba was to split the Muslims and spread anarchy in the Islamic society. He Provoked Muslims to kill Uthman(R.A) since he assumed that Uthman(R.A) had occupied the seat of Ali(A.S). He was also the primary source of mischief and revolution during the reign of Ali(A.S). During Ali's(A.S) caliphate, there was certainly bloodshed among Muslims, but it should also be remembered that whenever Ali(A.S) saw a good opportunity to avoid bloodshed, he restrained for the benefit of the Muslim nation. Ali(A.S) had strong beliefs that he should not start a war with other Muslims, but his army did not retreat when the enemy started it. He ordered his soldiers not to kill those who would be injured, or could not defend themselves or escape from the battlefield and not to hurt women.

The Caliphate of Ali(A.S) did not comprise new conquer but was characterized by civil and cultural accomplishments such as; police organization, constructing the court of arbitration, and building jails. Besides that, Ali(A.S) transferred the capital of Caliphate from Madinah to Kufah in Iraq, due to its strategic position in the mid of the Islamic empire at that time. Kufah thrived as the schools of jurisprudence and grammar were established. In addition, Ali(A.S) gave his orders to furnish the letters of the Holy Qur'an with vowel signs for the first time.

Martyrdom

On the 19th of Ramadan, while Ali(A.S) was praying fajr prayer in the Koufa mosque, a man named 'ibn Muljam' attacked him with his sword covered with poison. An elder from the Quraish reported that when Ibn Muljam struck Ali(A.S), he said:

"I have succeeded by the Lord of the Ka'ba."

Ali(A.S) lived for two days wounded by the poisoned sword. He ordered his sons not to kill the group of people, as the act was committed by only one member of the Kharijite group and not all of them.

During these two days, he dictated his will to his house:

"I advise you not to consider anyone as a partner of the Lord, be firm in your belief that there is one and only one God, i.e., Allah. Do not waste the knowledge that the Prophet Muhammad ﷺ gave you, and do not give up and destroy his Sunnah [traditions]. Keep these two pillars of Islam [the monotheism and the Sunnah] and act on my advice."

He embraced martyrdom on the 21st of Ramadan in the city of Kufa in 661 CE. His Caliphate remained for five and a half years. Imam Hasan (A.S) led the funeral prayer for him and also take Qisas later by killing ibn Muljam.

May Allah have mercy on Ali Ibn Abi Talib (A.S) and be pleased with him and assemble us among his company. A.M.E.E.N.

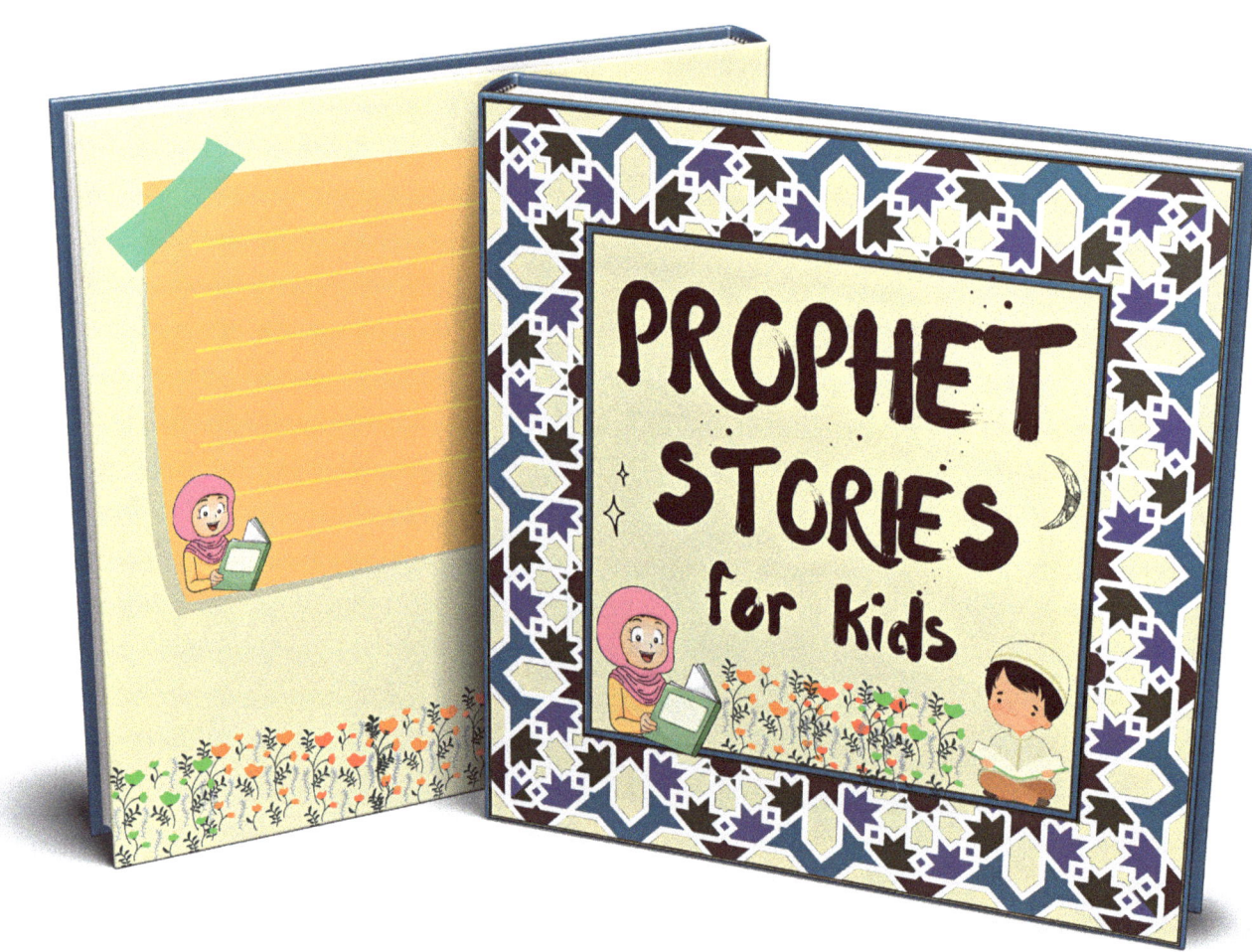

ISBN 978-1-990544-43-9

*Search ISBN on the retailer website

Premium Color Pages Hardcover

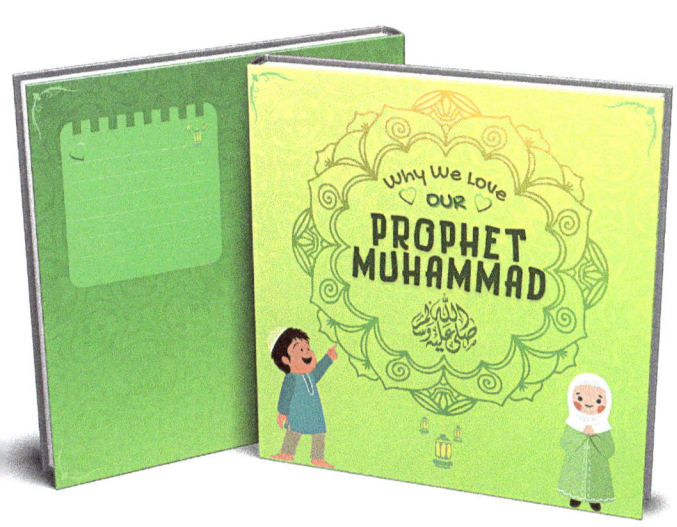

ISBN 978-1-990544-42-2

ISBN 978-1-990544-41-5

ISBN 978-1-990544-45-3

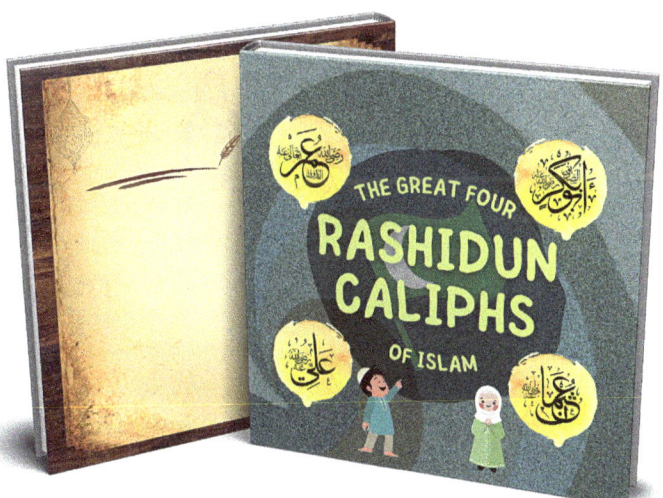

ISBN 978-1-990544-44-6

*Search ISBN on the retailer website